Donated by
Jacquelyn C. Miller
In Loving Memory of Her
Husband, Bruce.

Mysterious Encounters

Atlantis

by Stuart A. Kallen

KIDHAVEN PRESS
A part of Gale, Cengage Learning

GALE
CENGAGE Learning™

Detroit • New York • San Francisco • New Haven, Conn • Waterville, Maine • London

LIBRARY OF CONGRESS CATALOGING-IN-PUBLICATION DATA

Kallen, Stuart A., 1955-
  Atlantis / by Stuart A. Kallen.
      p. cm. -- (Mysterious encounters)
  Includes bibliographical references and index.
  ISBN 978-0-7377-5534-3 (hardcover)
  1. Atlantis (Legendary place)--Juvenile literature. I. Title.
GN751.K35 2011
398.23'4--dc22

2010047342

KidHaven Press
27500 Drake Rd.
Farmington Hills, MI 48331

ISBN-13: 978-0-7377-5534-3
ISBN-10: 0-7377-5534-2

Printed in the United States of America
1 2 3 4 5 6 7 15 14 13 12 11

Printed by Bang Printing, Brainerd, MN, 1st Ptg., 03/2011

Contents

Chapter 1

A Legendary Land

In 2007, the cartoon character SpongeBob SquarePants appeared in the animated movie *SpongeBob's Atlantis SquarePantis*. In the cartoon, the famous animated sea sponge searches for the world's largest bubble in a land called Atlantis. *SpongeBob's Atlantis SquarePantis* is just one of many cartoons and films that have been made about the **mythical** Atlantis. The lost island has been featured in dozens of movies and TV series and thousands of books. The first recorded tale of Atlantis was written by Greek poet and **philosopher** Plato more than 2,300 years ago. This story, still read today, has caused centuries of speculation and wonder.

Plato's Atlantis

Sometime around 355 B.C., Plato described Atlantis as an ancient civilization that existed around 9600 B.C. According to Plato, Atlantis was one of the most powerful countries on Earth. The nation's noble people, called Atlanteans, dwelled in cities filled with magnificent palaces and temples. However, Atlantis did not survive. A disaster struck, and the island vanished without a trace.

Plato's haunted story of Atlantis appeared in *Timaeus* and *Critias*, a pair of essays called **dialogs**. A dialog is an essay that has a conversation between two or more people.

A sculpture depicts Plato, the Greek poet and philosopher who wrote about the ancient civilization of Atlantis more than 2,300 years ago.

Plato describes the foods grown on Atlantis:

Whatever fragrant things there now are in the earth, whether roots, or herbage, or woods, or essences which distil from fruit and flower, grew and thrived in that land; also ... drinks and meats and ointments, and a good store of chestnuts and the like ... all these that sacred island ... brought forth fair and wondrous and in infinite abundance.

Quoted in Eberhard Zangger, *The Flood From Heaven*. New York: William Morrow, 1992, p. 29.

Plato's dialogs were imaginary discussions between several philosophers and the Greek poet and politician named Solon, who died around 558 B.C. Solon says he was told of the mythical land of Atlantis by an Egyptian priest named Senchis.

Plato's dialogs describe the history of Atlantis that had been passed down by word of mouth from generation to generation. By writing down the oral history, Plato recorded details of a story that is still talked about today.

The Pillars of Hercules

In *Timaeus,* Senchis tells Solon that the great island of Atlantis was located in the Atlantic Ocean in front of the Pillars of Hercules. In ancient times, the Pillars of Hercules was the name given to the column-like rocks at the Strait of Gibraltar (jih-BRAWL-ter). This narrow strait, or waterway, is where the Mediterranean Sea meets the Atlantic Ocean. The strait separates Spain in Europe from Morocco in Africa.

The priest told Solon that Atlantis was a huge island, larger than "Libya and Asia put together."[1] In Plato's day, this would have been a surprising statement. At that time, Libya was believed to be the entire area of land west of Egypt that makes up most of northern Africa. This area is as big as Europe. Asia also was thought to be a giant landmass. The Greeks believed Asia included the present-day Middle East, eastern Europe, India, and China. This area of land is itself larger than the entire Atlantic Ocean where Atlantis was said to be located.

The short sentence that mentions the Pillars of Hercules, Libya, and Asia has been the source of countless arguments over the centuries. Some believe Senchis was describing the North American continent, the location of the present-day United States and Canada. However, this area was unknown to Egyptians until the 15th century A.D. Another **theory** states that Senchis was simply de-

A map shows one interpretation of how Plato described the location of Atlantis, off the coast of Spain between Europe and North America.

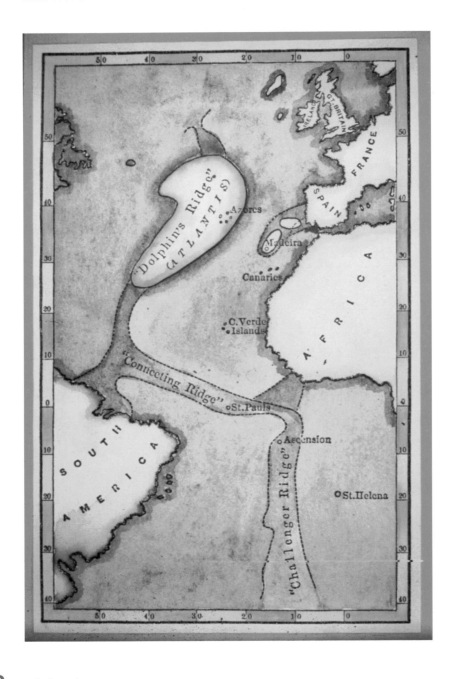

scribing a place that was beyond the reach of the small ships used in ancient times. Scientist Eberhard Zangger explains: "Traditionally, the pillars of Hercules marked the end of the known world—to venture beyond them was a symbol for going beyond the limits of man."[2]

The Land of Poseidon

No matter where Atlantis was located, it was described in Plato's dialogs as a magically beautiful world. The island was said to have been created by the Greek sea god Poseidon (poh-SIGH-duhn). This powerful **deity** (dee-UH-tee), or god, created Atlantis as a gift, to show his love to a mortal woman named Cleito. Poseidon formed Atlantis as a citadel, or round fort, on a mountaintop where

A drawing imagines Atlantis as Plato described it, with a citadel on top of a mountain surrounded by rings of water and land.

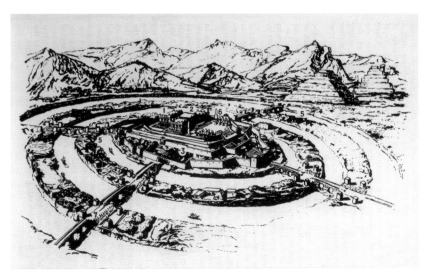

Cleito lived. To protect Cleito in the citadel, Poseidon surrounded it by rings of water and land. In his dialog Plato described how Poseidon created the island:

> He fortified the mountain on which [Cleito] lived by ... making alternate circles of sea and land, first small circles, then larger and larger, two of land, three of sea, around the center of the island ... so that the mountain [where Cleito lived] was inaccessible to man.[3]

Living together on the mountaintop, Poseidon and Cleito had five pairs of twin boys. The first born of the first set of twins was named Atlas and the is-

How Big Was Atlantis?

Plato said the royal capi of Atlantis was about 340 by 227 miles (547 by 365km) in size. Nine other towns of similar size were said to occupy the island. If true, this would make Atlantis about 3,400 by 2,270 miles (5,472 by 3,653km), more than one and a half times the size of the United States. Historians doubt such a large landmass ever existed in the Atlantic Ocean.

land of Atlantis and the Atlantic Ocean were named after him. Atlas was the first king of Atlantis and he ruled the land with his nine brothers. The offspring of these men ruled Atlantis for many generations.

King Atlas built a temple on the mountaintop in the center of Atlantis to honor his father. In the middle of the temple stood a giant, solid-gold statue of Poseidon riding a chariot. The chariot was pulled by winged horses. The costly statue was among many of the treasures in the kingdom. As Plato wrote, Atlantis possessed "riches as had never been amassed before in any kingdom nor will easily be found again."[4]

A Rich and Beautiful Land

According to legend, Atlantis was rich in natural resources. There were large reserves of gold, silver, and precious stones there as well as vast forests that provided timber for building. The island terrain was dotted with lush meadows, ponds, lakes, rivers, small villages, and quaint hamlets. These wild areas attracted a large collection of wild and domestic animals, including elephants.

The Atlanteans built a variety of temples and royal palaces from precious metals and ivory made from elephant tusks. Plato describes the glorious temple of Poseidon: "The exterior of the temple they coated with silver, save only the pinnacles [upright posts], and these they covered with gold. As to the interior, they made the roof all of ivory in ap-

The Temple of Poseidon at Atlantis is depicted as beautiful and richly decorated. The temple was made from ivory, gold, and silver, as described by Plato.

pearance, [and decorated it with] gold and silver.[5]

Drunk with Pride

Surrounded by wealth and abundance, the Atlanteans lived simple, virtuous lives. Plato writes, "Their hearts were true and in all ways noble, and they showed gentleness joined with wisdom ... in their dealings with one another. ... [Their] wealth did not make them drunk with pride so that they lost control of themselves and went to ruin."[6]

Eventually, the Atlanteans did become drunk with pride and grew selfish and mean. Plato writes that their greed made them "ugly to look upon ... filled as they were with lawless ambition and power."[7] Zeus (zooce), the most powerful of all Greek gods, looked down on Atlantis from his throne in the heavens and did not like what he saw. Zeus gathered together all the other gods in a great council and asked the deities to pass judgment on the people. The gods decided the Atlanteans should be punished for their greed, so they destroyed Atlantis with violent earthquakes and floods. According to Senchis, the entire island of Atlantis was "swallowed by the sea and vanished in a single dreadful day and in a single dreadful night."[8]

A Moral Lesson

Plato's description of Atlantis and its people was written more than 2,300 years ago. It fills little more than twenty pages, but the moral lesson of the story is universal. A beautiful land was destroyed by the sea when its people lost their virtue, or goodness.

There is no proof Atlantis ever existed but scientists and scholars have sought to answer questions about the land and its people for centuries. Some believe the Atlanteans had superhuman powers. Others think that the country was a small island where just a few people lived. Whatever the case, the search for Atlantis continues and the lost land lives on in the minds of millions today.

Chapter 2

Atlantis Reborn

In 1623, the famed English scientist and philosopher Francis Bacon wrote a book based on the story of Atlantis. Bacon's *The New Atlantis* was about a mythical island where people were kind, generous, intelligent, and spiritual, or religious. Bacon's novel was one of the first books to mention Atlantis since Plato completed *Timaeus* and *Critias* in 355 B.C. *The New Atlantis* was one of the few stories written about the legendary island, and the general public remained largely unaware of the Atlantis story. That changed in 1882 when the politician and author Ignatius Donnelly published *Atlantis: The Antediluvian World*.

Antediluvian (an-tee-dill-OOH-vee-an) means

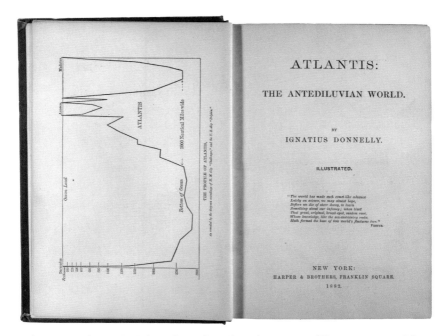

The popular 1882 book *Atlantis: The Antediluvean World* by Ignatius Donnelly made the tale of Atlantis widely known in the United States.

ancient or prehistoric. In *Atlantis: The Antediluvian World*, Donnelly carefully studied Plato's descriptions of ancient Atlantean architecture, geography, natural resources, and society. He analyzed every word and sentence of Plato's short text that described the mythical island. After careful study, Donnelly came to believe that Atlantis was real and the people of the island gave birth to modern civilization.

A Sensible History

At the time Donnelly wrote *Atlantis: The Antediluvian World*, the United States was a growing nation. Millions of immigrants were moving to America from Europe and elsewhere to build new lives. In describing Plato's Atlantis, Donnelly used terms that would be easily understood by plain-spoken 19th-century Americans:

> There are in Plato's [story] no marvels; no myths; no tales of [or monsters such as] gorgons, hobgoblins, or giants. It is a plain and reasonable history of a people who built temples, ships, and canals; who lived by agriculture and commerce; who, in pursuit of trade, reached out to all countries around them. ... [We] see an immigrant [Poseidon] enter the country, marry one of the native women [Cleito], and settle down, in time, a great nation grows up around him.[9]

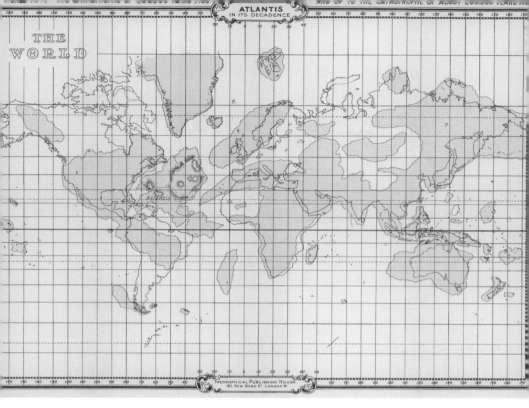

A map shows Atlantis as forming a land bridge between Europe and the Americas, which Donnelly claimed allowed Atlanteans to travel among the continents to share ancient knowledge with the New World.

A Land Bridge

Donnelly believed that Atlanteans extended their empire from Europe, across the Atlantic Ocean, to the Americas. He wrote that Atlantis was at one time connected to Europe and the Americas by a long, narrow land bridge called a plateau (pla-TOW) that stretched across the Atlantic Ocean. Using the land bridge, Atlanteans traveled to South, Central, and North America bringing knowledge from ancient Egypt to the New World. He claimed that proof of this could be seen in the Egyptian pyramids as well as in pyramids built in Central America by the Maya Indians. Donnelly asserted that the great pyramids of Egypt were planned and built by people from Atlantis. The Egyptian pyramid designs were then taken to Central America by Atlanteans. These plans were shared with the Mayan people, who used them to build similar pyramids, as the story goes.

Donnelly believed that the Atlantis land bridge was destroyed by a great volcanic eruption combined with an earthquake. This caused the plateau to sink into the ocean in a single day. The only landforms that remained were the highest mountain peaks. These tall ridges poke out of the ocean to form the Caribbean islands of Cuba and Bermuda.

The Great Flood

Donnelly shocked some readers by comparing the tale of Atlantis to stories in the Bible. He wrote that the tale of Noah's ark is actually based on the great deluge of Atlantis. The Bible reads, "The windows of heaven were opened and the rain was upon the earth forty days and forty nights. ... And ... all the high hills, that were under the whole heaven, were covered."[10]

Donnelly asserts Noah's story is similar to the Mayan creation myth, called the *Popol Vuh*, which states, "The waters were agitated by the will of [the gods], and a great [flood] came. ... [People] were engulfed ... the face of the earth was obscured [hidden], and a heavy darkening rain commenced—rain by day and rain by night."[11]

Donnelly goes on to describe flood stories told by Native Americans in the United States and Canada. He concludes that all these stories were spread around the globe by Atlanteans who had managed to escape the great flood that destroyed their island.

Donnelly finds many similarities between the people living in the Americas, Europe, and Atlantis. He writes: "If we find on both sides of the Atlantic precisely the same arts, sciences, religious beliefs, habits, customs, and traditions, it is absurd to say that the peoples of the two continents arrived separately at precisely the same ends."[12]

The Atlantis Craze

Donnelly's theories are not believed by modern historians who point out that the events he describes happened in different centuries. While Plato said Atlantis existed in 12,000 B.C., it is known that the Egyptian pyramids were built around 8,800 years later in 3200 B.C. The Mayan pyramids, such as El Castillo (el cah-STEE-yo) in Chichen Itza (CHEE-chen EET-zah), Mexico, were constructed much more recently, sometime between the 9th and 12th centuries A.D. In addition, stories about a great deluge are common to almost every culture on earth.

In the 19th century, however, few people understood the history of ancient civilizations in the Americas or Egypt. When *Atlantis: The Antediluvian World* was published, Donnelly's theories were taken as fact. The book became a best seller, making its author a wealthy international celebrity.

Donnelly became the leading authority of what was known as **Atlantology**, or the study of Atlantis. This fad was popular for about ten years in the United States, England, Germany, France, Russia,

and elsewhere. In Great Britain, Prime Minister William Gladstone was so excited by *Atlantis: The Antediluvian World* that he personally wrote Donnelly a letter of praise. Gladstone even asked his government for money to build a ship to search for the sunken island of Atlantis. His request was denied.

In the years since Donnelly wrote *Atlantis: The Antediluvian World* many people have searched

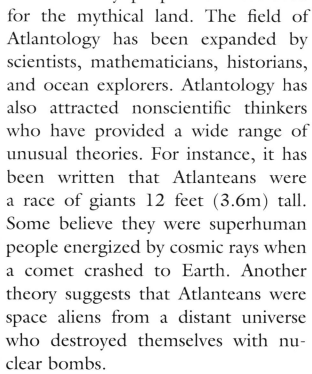

for the mythical land. The field of Atlantology has been expanded by scientists, mathematicians, historians, and ocean explorers. Atlantology has also attracted nonscientific thinkers who have provided a wide range of unusual theories. For instance, it has been written that Atlanteans were a race of giants 12 feet (3.6m) tall. Some believe they were superhuman people energized by cosmic rays when a comet crashed to Earth. Another theory suggests that Atlanteans were space aliens from a distant universe who destroyed themselves with nuclear bombs.

A painting depicts a scuba diver exploring the ruins of Atlantis on the ocean floor. Donnelly's book sparked interest in searching for the lost civilzation among scientists, historians, and other enthusiasts.

The man whose book started all this speculation believed Atlanteans were ordinary humans who created an advanced civilization over thousands of years. Donnelly wrote:

> They were the founders of nearly all our arts and sciences; they were the parents of our fundamental beliefs; they were the first civilizers, the first navigators, the first merchants, the first colonizers of earth. ... This lost people were our ancestors, their blood flows in our veins. ... Every line of race and thought, of blood and belief, leads back to them.[13]

Atlantis: No Way, No How, No Where

According to skeptic Kevin Christopher, "There is no evidence whatsoever to indicate that Atlantis represented any real place at any time. ... All of the evidence points to the story being one of Plato's noble lies: useful fictions used to make a point, not to refer to the past."

Kevin Christopher, "Atlantis: No Way, No How, No Where," The Committee for Skeptical Inquiry, September 2001. www.csicop.org/sb/show/atlantis_no_way_no_how_no_where.

Chapter 3

Occult Atlantis

During the last part of the 19th century, interest in the **occult**, or magic, peaked in the United States and Europe. Millions of average people learned to conduct séances (SAY-on-sez) to try to talk to the dead. Some peered into crystal balls to see into the future. Others cast magic spells to ward off evil or attract love or money.

Those who believed in the occult were called spiritualists. By the 1890s, over 8 million Americans claimed to be spiritualists. These believers wrote and printed their own newspapers and joined together into organizations. One of the major spiritualist groups in New York City was called the Theosophical Society. The society was founded in

1875 by a Russian immigrant named Helena Blavatsky, known as Madam Blavatsky.

A Wild Waste of Waters

Blavatsky was a well-known New York **medium**, or a person who claims to understand and deliver messages from spirits that exist in the afterlife. Blavatsky's connection to Atlantis begins with the belief that the world is run by what she calls the secret order of cosmic masters. To her, the cosmic masters included Jesus and Plato. She believed that thousands of years ago the cosmic masters traveled to Earth from a distant planet in outer space. The cosmic masters, Blavatsky thought, then moved to Atlantis where they founded an advanced civilization.

In 1877, Blavatsky wrote a 1,200-page book called *Isis Unveiled*. In the work, she states that all of the world's major

Madam Blavatsky claimed in her writings that the citizens of Atlantis were the key source of wisdom and knowledge for people in the modern world.

religions are based on common ancient wisdom. According to Blavatsky, this wisdom came from Atlantis and could provide all the answers to questions about life on earth. Blavatsky writes:

> At different epochs [times] of the past, huge islands, and even continents, existed where now there is but a wild waste of waters. In these submerged temples and libraries the archaeologist would find. ... The materials for filling in all the gaps that now exist in what we imagine is history.[14]

Blavatsky published *Isis Unveiled* five years before Ignatius Donnelly wrote his best-selling *Atlantis: The Antediluvian World*. Historians believe Blavatsky inspired Donnelly's theories, but her book was not as popular as his. Several years after Donnelly inspired the "Atlantis craze," Blavatsky wrote another book called *The Secret Doctrine* that discussed Atlantis.

Sons of Light and Darkness

According to *The Secret Doctrine,* the Golden Age of Atlantis occurred about 1 million years ago. During this time, 2 million people lived in the capi of Atlantis. According to Blavatsky, "In those days of old ... the gods walked the earth, and mixed freely with the mortals."[15] Blavatsky claims the Atlanteans were giants. They traveled about the world in air-

A painting shows the destruction of Atlantis. Blavatsky claimed that some Atlanteans known as the Sons of Light and Wisdom escaped the civilization's demise and settled in Tibet.

ships powered by a mysterious fluid called vril. The Atlantean military filled giant airships with soldiers to wage war on other nations, Blavatsky says in the book. These airships dropped bombs filled with poison gas while soldiers shot at enemies with fire-tipped arrows.

Blavatsky says the Atlanteans began practicing black magic in 850,000 B.C. They changed from what she called the Sons of Light and Wisdom to the Sons of Darkness. The Sons of Darkness used black magic to create creatures called chimeras (KIE-meer-ahs) that were part human, part animal. These creatures had the bodies of humans and the heads of tigers, bears, and other vicious beasts. On the battlefield they killed enemies and ate their bodies.

Some Sons of Light, also called white magicians, opposed the Sons of Darkness. These groups fought one another for centuries. Finally, Atlantis was submerged by a gigantic earthquake in 9564 B.C. Some Sons of Light were able to escape to the Himalayas, a mountain range in Tibet, where they continued to influence the human race.

A Magic Crystal from Atlantis

Madam Blavatsky died in 1891 but in the early 1900s, another public figure arose to take Blavatsky's place as the leading celebrity spiritualist in the United States. Edgar Cayce was born in Kentucky in 1877. When he was only nineteen years old, Cayce began having visions that allowed him to give "life readings" to his followers. During a reading, Cayce would enter into a trance and

The Magical Fire Stone

Edgar Cayce believed that more information about the magical Fire Stone of Atlantis will one day be found hidden in three different locations: in the ocean near Bimini in the Bahamas, in the ruins of an ancient temple in Yucatan, Mexico, and buried near the Sphinx in Egypt.

would reveal details of a person's health, dreams, and deepest thoughts. During his trance sessions, Cayce often discussed Atlantis.

Cayce said the island of Atlantis stretched from Gibraltar (at the southern end of the Iberian Peninsula and entrance to the Mediterranean Sea) to the Gulf of Mexico. The Atlanteans possessed a magic crystal called the Tuaoi Stone, or Fire Stone. This stone could focus the natural energies of the sun, the moon, and powers of the earth. The power of the Fire Stone is explained by occult researcher Joseph Robert Jochmans: "Currents of energy were transmitted [by the Fire Stone] throughout the land, like radio waves, and, powered by these, crafts and vehicles traversed the land, through the sky and under the sea at the speed of sound."[16]

The Fire Stone could also be used to heat and light buildings and transmit pictures and voices over great distances. However, the Atlanteans misused the powers of the Fire Stone by turning it into a death ray. This caused a massive explosion that set off a chain of volcanic eruptions, destroying Atlantis in 10,000 B.C.

The Ancient Atlantean Warrior

Although Cayce was very popular, he was largely forgotten after his death in 1945. This situation changed in the late 1960s when there was a renewed interest in the occult as a result of the New Age movement. New Age believers engage in prac-

Judith Zebra Knight became famous in the mid-1980s for claiming that she was able to channel the spirit of an Atlantean warrior named Ramtha. This claim earned her both followers who wanted to learn from Ramtha's teachings and critics who didn't believe her claims.

tices such as telling fortunes, casting magic spells, and conducting séances. Some are known as channelers, people who **channel**, or act as a pathway, for messages delivered by spirits.

One of the best-known channelers is Judith Zebra (JZ) Knight. She became a New Age celebrity in 1985 when she began channeling an Atlantean warrior named Ramtha. According to Knight, "I leave my own body, go through [a] ... tunnel of white light and all the while Ramtha has utilized my body for his teachings."[17] When Ramtha appears, Knight begins speaking in the gruff, male voice of the spirit who says he lived 35,000 years ago.

Antarctica Is Atlantis

According to Knight, Ramtha was born in a lost land called Lemuria located in the Pacific Ocean. Lemuria was ruled by Atlantis but Ramtha led an army of 2.5 million soldiers to conquer the Atlanteans. Ramtha stayed in Atlantis, where he learned ancient mysteries from an unnamed god and became enlightened. In a 2008 interview, Knight revealed the location of Atlantis, which, she says, is reappearing due to the modern problem of global warming:

> Atlantis was and is in part of Antarctica [the South Pole]. It has been predicted that it will rise or surface again… [because] the ice is melting from the mountains and valleys of Antarctica due to global warming. The monuments of ancient cities will soon be seen. Antarctica is the ancient Atlantis.[18]

Hollywood stars such as Shirley MacLaine and Linda Evans have paid Knight up to $1,500 for personal sessions with Ramtha. In 2008, it was estimated that Knight earned about $10 million a year selling books, CDs, DVDs, candles, posters, jewelry, and other Ramtha-related items. This has led skeptic Robert T. Carroll to write, "It is not clear why Ramtha would choose [to speak through] Knight, but it is very clear why Knight would choose Ramtha: fame and fortune, or simple delusion."[19]

Like Cayce, Blavatsky, and countless others, Knight appeals to the public's hunger for ancient wisdom. As long as people desire magic in their lives, Atlantis will be discussed as a source of occult powers. Channelers and mediums will obtain fame and fortune with Atlantean tales of giants, warriors, and stones of fire.

Chapter 4

The Thera Theories

There are many theories about the reality of Atlantis. While some say no such place ever existed, others link Atlantis to real locations all over the globe. Books have been written placing Atlantis in present-day Iceland or Sweden. It has also been said Atlantis was really in the islands called the Azores, which are in the Atlantic Ocean, 930 miles (1500km) west of Portugal. Some have concluded Atlantis was in the Caribbean, on islands such as the Bahamas, Cuba, or Bimini (BIH-mih-nee). Others guess that Atlantis was located in Tibet, Central America, Indonesia, or even Northern California.

A Maze of Rooms

When Plato described Atlantis, he could not have known about the existence of Iceland, the Caribbean, or the Americas. Those areas had yet to be discovered. Therefore, some who have studied Atlantis try to place the lost land in the world known to Plato and the ancient Greeks. Those people believe Atlanteans really lived on a Greek island now called Santorini (san-tor-EE-nee). This island is located about 120 miles (193km) southeast of mainland Greece in the Aegean Sea, which is part of the Mediterranean. About 4,000 years ago, Santorini was called Thera. Facts that support the idea that Atlantis was located on Santorini are called the Thera theories.

The Thera theories first evolved after 1900

The remains of an alabaster throne found at the Palace of Knossos is "guarded" by a pair of griffins painted on a mural behind it.

when a British **archaeologist** (ar-kee-AHL-uh-jist) named Arthur Evans visited the island of Crete, 70 miles (112km) south of Santorini. Evans was on Crete looking for ruins left by ancient civilizations when he discovered remarkable treasures. At a site called Knossos (KNO-sohs), Evans unearthed a huge building now known as the Knossos Palace. The structure has over one thousand rooms connected by winding passages and staircases. The maze of rooms served as workshops, apartments, temples, and offices of a lost civilization.

In a large room called the Throne Sanctuary, Evans was struck by the exotic and unique nature of what he had discovered. A large throne carved out of the white mineral called alabaster overlooks a sunken area. The wall behind the throne features a painting of two griffins. These legendary creatures have the body of a lion and the head of an eagle.

The Wealthy Minoans

Although little was known about the people of Knossos at the time, Evans named them Minoans (mih-NO-ans). The name comes from a mythical king named Minos who was the son of the god Zeus. In the years following Evans's discovery, new discoveries at Knossos allowed scholars to understand the world of the ancient Minoans.

The Minoans were at the center of a thriving trade among Africa, Europe, and Asia. Trading made the island's 100,000 people very wealthy. The Minoans traded in wine, olive oil, spices, gold, and silver. They obtained great amounts of tin and copper, which were melted together to make bronze. The bronze was then used to make tools, jewelry, and artwork.

Bull Dancers

The Knossos Palace was built between 2600 and 2000 B.C. All roads on the island led to the palace, which was the center of Minoan life and culture. Paintings on the palace walls reveal that women held powerful positions in society. The Minoan religion was centered on female deities and ser-

A mural found in the ruins of the Palace of Knossos shows Minoans participating in the dangerous bull dance.

vices were conducted by women priests. According to historian Rodney Castleden, "The men in the murals were proud of bearing, yet subservient [less important] to the high-status women."[20]

Although Minoan deities were almost all female, the people also worshiped a male god called the Earthshaker. This deity was a combination of a bull and the sun. At festivals dedicated to the Earthshaker, both men and women perform the Minoan bull dance. This dangerous activity, depicted on murals, involves jumping over a live bull, grabbing its horns, and spinning a summersault over its back.

Connection to Atlantis

Plato wrote that the people of Atlantis were bull

worshippers who participated in bull jumping. Decades after Knossos was discovered, historians made a connection between the Atlanteans, Minoans on Crete, and the people of Thera.

In 1939, Greek archaeologist Spyridon Marinatos discovered evidence of a major volcanic eruption on the island of Thera in 1500 B.C. Marinatos concluded that at the time, Thera and Crete were a single large island. The volcano and resulting tidal wave caused the center of the island to collapse into the sea. According to Marinatos, "A terrible disaster struck. ... Cities, monumental structures and two of the three palaces were destroyed for all time."[21]

If an earthquake wiped out a civilization that

The Minos Maze

In Greek legend, King Minos ordered the construction of a labyrinth, or maze. The wandering paths in the labyrinth were meant to contain the mythical Minotaur, a creature that was half man, half bull. Because of the maze-like rooms at the Knossos Palace, Arthur Evans named the people who built it Minoans, or the people of King Minos.

An engraving shows a volcano erupting on Thera in 1866. An similar eruption around 1500 B.C. is thought to have given the island its unique horseshoe shape and may have resulted in the destruction of Krossus and the Minoan civilization.

was at the center of trade and culture in the ancient world, the Egyptians would have been aware of it. Perhaps the Egyptian priest who spoke of Atlantis in Plato's dialogs was recalling this disaster. This idea is explored by Atlantis expert Daniel Fleck. He says, "After the volcanic eruption, the Egyptians ... never again heard anything about the Minoans. As a result, they created a nice myth of a superior empire that provoked its own doom by the unbelievable arrogance [self-importance] ... of its population."[22]

Amazing Luxuries

After Marinatos published his theories in 1939, scientists continued to explore the region. In 1967, archaeologists on Santorini unearthed another amazing lost city that added proof to the Thera theories. Around 2000 B.C. a city called Akrotiri, was filled with large homes that contained amazing luxuries. Buildings had advanced plumbing and sewage systems. Ceramic pipes throughout the city provided hot and cold running water to toilets, bathtubs, showers, and sinks. This discovery fitted Plato's description of Atlanteans who had ways of "bringing up two springs of water from beneath the earth, in gracious plenty flowing ... fountains, one of cold and another of hot water. ... [There] were the king's bath and also the baths of private persons."[23]

Homes in Akrotiri contained other signs of great wealth including pottery, furniture, and tools. Many beautiful paintings were also found. The paintings were of Minoan fishermen, women gathering spices, jumping blue monkeys, and ships at sea. The pottery at the Akrotiri site was identical to pottery unearthed at Knossos. This led archaeologist Peter James to write:

> Thera was closely linked to ... the great palaces on

An excavation site on Santorini reveals a building from the city of Akrotiri, which was discovered in 1969. Some scientists exploring the ruins think that Akrotiri is connected to Knossos and Plato's descriptions of Atlantis.

Crete. [The pottery] thus seemed to confirm [Marinatos's] theory that the palaces were destroyed by tidal waves and ash-falls from Thera's eruption. It was a scenario dramatic enough to match Plato's Atlantis. While Crete itself had not sunk, the central [part] of Thera had, and its settlements had been engulfed in a mountain of ash and lava.[24]

After this discovery in 1969, three books were written stating Atlantis and Thera were one and the same. Since that time, many have come to believe that the highly advanced, wealthy Minoans were really Plato's Atlanteans. However, another interesting theory has been developed. Some say that the Minoans read Plato's story and were trying to imitate the mythical Atlanteans. This would have led Thera's neighbors to believe the Minoans were very powerful when in fact they were a small society on a tiny island.

An Unfinished Tale

For reasons unknown Plato never finished writing his tale of Atlantis. It is an unfinished story, much like the continuing search for Atlantis. People have been hunting for the mythical land for centuries. And it seems for some, the search for Atlantis will never end.

Notes

Chapter 1: A Legendary Land

1. Quoted in Andrew Collins, *Gateway to Atlantis*. New York: Carroll & Graf, 2000, p. 28.
2. Eberhard Zangger, *The Flood from Heaven*. New York: William Morrow, 1992, p. 109.
3. Quoted in Otto Muck, *The Secrets of Atlantis*. New York: Times Books, 1978, p. 6.
4. Quoted in Muck, *The Secrets of Atlantis*, p. 7.
5. Quoted in Zangger, *The Flood from Heaven*, p. 30.
6. Quoted in Zangger, *The Flood from Heaven*, p. 35.
7. Quoted in Zangger, *The Flood from Heaven*, p. 36.
8. Quoted in Muck, *The Secrets of Atlantis*, p. 6.

Chapter 2: Atlantis Reborn

9. Ignatius Donnelly, *Atlantis: The Antediluvian World*. New York: Gramercy, 1949, p. 20.
10. Quoted in Donnelly, *Atlantis*, p. 86.
11. Quoted in Donnelly, *Atlantis*, p. 86.
12. Donnelly, *Atlantis*, p. 111.
13. Donnelly, *Atlantis*, p. 324.

Chapter 3: Occult Atlantis

14. Quoted in James Bramwell, *Lost Atlantis*. New York: Harper and Brothers, 1938, p. 193.
15. H.P. Blavatsky, "The Secret Doctrine," Theosophical University Press Online Edition, 2010. www.theosociety

.org/pasadena/sd/sd2-1-15.htm.

16. Joseph Robert Jochmans, "Edgar Cayce on the Great Crystal of Atlantis—and Beyond," Forgotten Ages Research, 2010.

17. Quoted in Michelene K. Bell, "Meet JZ Knight," In Light Times, 2010. www.inlightimes.com/archives/2008/09/f2.htm.

18. Quoted in Michelene K. Bell, "Meet JZ Knight."

19. Robert T. Carroll, "Ramtha (a.k.a. JZ KNIGHT)," Skeptic's Dictionary, 2009. www.skepdic.com/ramtha.html.

Chapter 4: The Thera Theories

20. Rodney Castleden, *Atlantis Destroyed*. London: Routledge, 1999, p. 25.

21. Quoted in Peter James, *The Sunken Kingdom*. London: Jonathan Cape, 1995, p. 64.

22. Daniel Fleck, "Thera-Crete," Atlantis: The Cradle of Civilization, 2006. www.atlantia.de/atlantis_english/myth/atlantis/atlantis_thera_crete.htm.

23. Quoted in Jeff Kurtti, *The Mythical World of Atlantis: Theories of the Lost Empire from Plato to Disney*. New York: Disney Editions, 2001, p. 37.

24. James, *The Sunken Kingdom*, p. 69.

Glossary

archaeologist: A person who studies archaeology, the unearthing and examining of the physical remains of ancient cultures.

Atlantology: The study of Atlantis.

channel: To act as a pathway for messages delivered by spirits.

deity: A god or goddess.

dialogs: Essays in which two or more characters are portrayed as holding a conversation.

medium: Someone who claims to deliver messages from spirits or ghosts that exist in the afterlife.

mythical: Based on myth or legend, rather than historical fact.

occult: Knowledge of the supernatural or magical.

philosopher: A person who studies philosophy, which concerns matters such as the meaning of life, learning, values, and reason.

theory: A concept formed by guesswork to explain an event of unknown origin.

For Further Exploration

Books

Jack DeMolay, *Atlantis: The Mystery of the Lost City*. New York: PowerKids Press, 2007. This book explores the facts and fiction behind the Atlantis story in the graphic novel form. Eye-catching artwork illustrates Plato's story, life of the Atlanteans, and possible locations of the lost city.

Anne Pearson, *Ancient Greece*. New York: DK, 2007. An informative guide to ancient Greece, where the story of Atlantis originated. In addition to discussing daily life, the book covers Greek gods, philosophers, and art.

Kathryn Walker, *The Mystery of Atlantis*. New York: Crabtree, 2010. This book follows several theories about Atlantis, where it might be, and whether it really existed.

Holly Wallace, *The Mystery of Atlantis*. Chicago: Heinemann Library, 2006. This is an examination of various Atlantis theories and scientific methods that have been used to find the location of the lost island.

Websites

Atlantis: The Cradle of Mankind (www.atlantia .de/atlantis_english/atlantis.htm). This site contains detailed information about different Atlantis myths. Pages feature maps and various theories as to the lost land's location.

The British School at Athens: Knossos (www.bsa .ac.uk/knossos/vrtour/throne/46_1.htm). This site offers a virtual 3-D tour of Knossos Palace on the isle of Crete where the Minoans once lived. Visitors can view the Throne Room, the Central Court, and other areas of this ancient ruin associated with Atlantis.

The Lost Continent: Atlantis (www.unmuseum .org/atlantis.htm). The story of Atlantis illustrated with beautiful renditions of Poseidon's temple, maps, and what the city might have looked like.

Index

Picture Credits

About the Author

Stuart A. Kallen is the author of more than 250 nonfiction books for children and young adults. He has written on topics ranging from the theory of relativity to the history of rock and roll. In addition, Mr. Kallen has written award-winning children's video and television scripts. In his spare time, he is a singer/songwriter/guitarist in San Diego.